RELIGIOUS THEMES IN FLOWER ARRANGEMENT

I. In the temple (page 38)

RELIGIOUS THEMES IN FLOWER ARRANGEMENT

BY RUTH E. MULLINS

Hearthside Press, Incorporated • *Publishers* • NEW YORK

ACKNOWLEDGMENTS

It is a pleasant obligation to express my appreciation through these pages to the following: Mrs. Fay McWhorter Mays, Fort Lauderdale, President of the Florida Federation of Garden Circles at the time this book was published, for her constructive and helpful criticism; Mrs. Vernon L. Conner, Mt. Dora, former President of the Florida Federation of Garden Circles, who has always been a source of inspiration in my work; and Mrs. P. Frankel Thau, Miami Beach, for her encouragement during the preparation of this book. Also to Mrs. Lillian P. Sutherland, Mrs. R. D. Rooks, Mrs. Mary Gardner, Mrs. Walter Rhulman, Mrs. Jack Crews, Mrs. Lawson Taylor, Mrs. Lewin Miskell, Mrs. Frank Jones, Mrs. Ivan Burry, Mrs. Thomas Gilbert and Mrs. R. C. Boothe, all of Fort Pierce, Florida. Dr. Jacob Philip Rudin, Rabbi of Temple Beth-El of Great Neck, New York, supplied the information on Jewish worship which is quoted in the text.

Many of my friends and former neighbors in West Virginia offered flowers, faith and encouragement. My thanks to Dr. and Mrs. Charles S. Runyan, Mr. W. E. Watson, Mrs. Myrtle B. Owens, and Mrs. E. E. Deitz, all of Pea Ridge Road in Huntington, and Mr. Arch Keller, Supervisor of Huntington Parks. I am grateful to Mrs. Inez Damewood, Mr. W. R. Jenni, Mr. C. Earl Mullins, Bertha of the Bertha Beauty Shop, Mr. Randy

Adkins, all of Charleston; Mrs. Ella Adkins and Mrs. Roy Adkins of Midkiff; Mr. and Mrs. Everett D. Adkins of Parkersburg; and Mrs. Myron B. Coffman of Ellanore.

A deeply felt *thank you* to the photographers: Mr. Vincent C. Stack of Fort Pierce for the series on the "Twenty-third Psalm"; Mr. Caryl White of Kent's Studio, DeLand, Florida, for the Easter and Church series; and Mr. George Kniska of the MaDell Studio in Huntington, West Virginia, who worked long hours to produce photographs of high quality. The color prints are his work, as are the majority of the black and whites.

And, finally, a very special acknowledgment to my husband, Major A. R. Mullins, Retired, who was my most loyal critic and adviser in the preparation of this manuscript.

CONTENTS

In The Beginning

In the beginning, on the second and third day of the creation, the Bible tells us that God created the waters and vegetation upon the earth. On the fifth day He created the birds and the creatures of the sea. On the sixth day He created man and gave him dominion over all things.

God looked upon His creation of beauty—not alone for the eye but for physical sustenance as well—and was well pleased. This with His spiritual leadership supplied body and soul requirements for luxurious and bountiful living which is our heritage.

From the dawn of history plant materials have played an important role as expression of joy in all religions of the world. Man is privileged to cut the physical beauties of God's flowering world and combine them into living pictures of a spiritual beauty to affirm and give outer symbol of his joy.

We speak of symbol—just what does the term imply? The word is derived from the Greek "sym" meaning *together* and *ballein* meaning *to throw*—hence the word "symbol" suggesting the throwing together or joining of an abstract idea and visible sign of it. In secular life a familiar example is the American flag. We salute it because the "Stars and Stripes" symbolize our United States.

The pagan nature worshipper was the first to attach particular significance to symbolism; to each deity (and there were many), he assigned a certain flower, fruit, or tree. In our work of arranging flowers to interpret religious themes, we can employ not only the religious symbols but the secular as well. In addition, we can draw on psychological impressions, using them alone or in combination with the other symbols. Lists of symbolism elsewhere in this book will be inspiring although they are not a complete record. Lack of space permits listing only those that are most easily understood and universally accepted. They exclude symbols that an arranger might choose to express some personally significant idea for which there is no universal emblem—such, for instance, as might be inspired by "swords into plowshares" from Isaiah 2:4. A sword handled to appear forged with a scythe or sickle would suggest the turning of war tools into implements of agriculture, the world's basic industry. This would be completely personal interpretation of *peace*, a message extracted from these ancient words.

For deeper and more reverent decoration in our worship centers, there is need for more thought and greater planning. Those whose duty it is to arrange flowers where man assembles to pay homage—in church, synagogue, cathedral, at any public gathering, or in the home—should train themselves in the use of suitable color, line, and form in plant materials. To this they should add a knowledge of appropriate symbolism.

In addition to the beauty a floral arrangement lends to decoration in a place of worship, it can become a medium of great value to an individual's growth in spiritual living, for it can be more than flowers in a vase, or perfection in technique or style. It is first and foremost a vision of beauty, but it can go beyond mere beauty; it can challenge the artist to see with his mind, interpret with his heart, and execute with his hands.

To be of spiritual value, an arrangement must come from within the designer. Its inception must originate within the soul of the artist. His performance, rendered with insight and feeling, will be in harmonious sympathy with God's beauty in spiritual life. Symbols of line, of shape, of color, of plant material, and in some cases of objects, are employed to result in vitalized expression. Because of man's strong emotional response to color, it is especially helpful in symbolizing the fruits of the spirit as set forth in Galatians 5:2: *love, joy, peace, longsuffering, gentleness, goodness, faith, meekness, temperance.*

Of course, any truly creative arrangement will leave much to the imagination of the observer. In interpreting religious themes with plant material, only major factors can be selected on which to center interest; it is expected that the viewer will mentally supply other details that may be part of an entire picture or idea. After all, if every detail is delineated in a picture, or an arrangement, or even a sermon, aesthetic or spiritual experience loses some of its appeal for the viewer or listener, because the important ingredient of audience participation is omitted.

The arrangements that follow are offered with the assumption that you, the reader, have a knowledge of the elements and principles of design, and of the technique in the selection and handling of plant material, container, and accessory if one is called for. In most cases, subtlety is avoided; the arrangements tell their stories in a direct and obvious language. None is intended as an end in itself, but merely as *one* way to impart a spiritual quality in interpreting a specific theme. It is hoped that with the reference lists offered, they will be enough to challenge the designing of compositions that will give emphasis to spiritual living. Symbols can be a main source of inspiration to quicken creative imagination along this line. As Christ Himself used symbols in His parables, let us employ them to deepen and enrich floral offerings to our Lord.

RELIGIOUS

THEMES IN

FLOWER

ARRANGEMENT

1

Great Religions
of the World

The ultimate goal of religious conviction is world brotherhood and peace, with ideals of understanding, tolerance, justice,
and love. This series of arrangements is presented with the
hope that it will arouse interest, stimulate thinking, and in-
crease our quest for a better knowledge of those who worship
in a form different from our own.

Only the highest and best ideals of the various religions are
interpreted. Naturally, in one arrangement, full justice cannot
be done to any one of them, but symbolism can interpret some
highlight or some festival which is a sacred part of a particular
doctrine.

Just as variety, color, and contrast bring out the best in
our international religious life, so, too, these qualities—variety,
color, contrast—are ingredients in the following arrangements.
It becomes the dedicated task of the arranger, as it is of the
writer, educator, minister, and any other who serves this
present age, to bring these properties together into a harmonious whole, working for the finished product of "Peace on earth;
Good will toward men."

HEAR, O ISRAEL, THE LORD OUR GOD, THE LORD IS ONE

(Book of Deuteronomy)

JUDAISM

Rosh Hashanah—Yom Kippur

The declaration of monotheism is absolutely central to the Jewish faith and it is regularly part of worship prayer services. Rosh Hashanah, celebrated on the early fall, is the Jewish New Year. It ushers in ten days of penitence, ending with Yom Kippur, the Day of Atonement. As in Bible times, so today, a main feature of the public worship is the blowing of the ram's horn (Shofar) which summons the people to obey the Word of God.

The "L" design is appropriate for this arrangement, largely because it so beautifully accommodates accessories of the ram's horn and the Torah which consists of the five books of Moses. Lovely fall colors are used with a white background.

Materials are dried dock, dahlias, chrysanthemums and small pieces of colored glass. The base is painted board.

THE SOUL IS NOT BORN, NOR DOES IT DIE . . . THE SOUL, SMALLER THAN THE SMALL AND GREATER THAN THE GREAT, IS HIDDEN IN THE HEARTS OF ALL LIVING CREATURES

(Katha Upanishad)

HINDUISM

The Reverence for Animals

The goal of the Hindu religion, practiced by the majority of the people of India, is a sublime one: to achieve union with the eternal spirit, called Brahma rather than God. Hinduism is not a sect but a complete way of life for all its followers. Since reincarnation in human or animal form is one of their beliefs, it is natural that Hindus should have deep compassion for all living creatures.

In the arrangement, serpentine lines thrusting forcefully upward and out are visually associated with snakes, one of the most marked features of Hinduism. The hand-carved accessory from India is also appropriate since the bird is held sacred. A marbleized white and black container and base are well suited in color and texture.

**IF A MAN SPEAKS OR ACTS WITH A PURE THOUGHT, HAPPINESS
FOLLOWS HIM, LIKE A SHADOW THAT NEVER LEAVES HIM**

Dhammapada (Way of the Law)

BUDDHISM

Wheel of the Law

Buddhism, one of the great Oriental religions, preaches
these "four noble Truths," revealed to Buddha in the Great
Enlightenment—that life means suffering, that suffering is
caused by desire, that when desire ends, suffering ends, and
that the way to end desire is to follow "the noble eightfold
path."

The Wheel of the Law, with its eight spokes representing
the eightfold path to perfection—Right Knowledge; Right In-
tention; Right Speech; Right Conduct; Right Means of Live-
lihood; Right Effort; Right Mindfulness; Right Concentra-
tion—is used here as an accessory. The Rikka form of Ikebana,
first used in Buddhist temples around 600 A.D., seemed appropriate for the arrangement. Lotus and magnolia leaves, dried
ginger, wood roses, locust, dried magnolia flower and seven
chrysanthemums are grouped using the seven different elements
of this ancient style.

NEVER DO TO OTHERS WHAT YOU WOULD NOT LIKE THEM DO TO YOU

Analects (The Confucian Bible)

CONFUCIANISM

Chinese Philosophy

Chinese ethics and religion are based to a large extent on the teachings of Confucius, whose wisdom was recorded by his disciples many centuries ago. His greatest precept can be equated with the Golden Rule: to do unto others as we would have them do to us.

Two Oriental figures are so placed in this arrangement as to suggest the natural position of a teacher to his student, or perhaps the relationship of man to man which is so basic to Chinese philosophy. Chinese appreciation of nature is expressed by the design which resembles a dwarfed tree in silhouette. The large circular hydrangeas, the curved line of the vase, and the round heads of the Chinese philosophers exemplify harmony through repetition of form. Hydrangeas, August lily (Hosta) foliage, and locust seed pods are arranged here in a Chinese antique vase with stand. Colors are white, green, and brown against a blue background.

TURN, THEREFORE, THY FACE TOWARDS THE HOLY TEMPLE OF MECCA; AND WHEREVER YE BE, TURN YOUR FACES TOWARDS THAT PLACE

The Koran

MOHAMMEDANISM

Turn Your Faces East

Islam is the youngest, the simplest, and perhaps the most explicit of the great religions. According to its followers, God revealed most of the sacred Koran to Mohammed during his life at Mecca, and for this reason prayer is said five times daily facing the city.

Here a kneeling figurine is turned towards an imaginary Mecca and gray weathered wood curves also in the same direction. Set against a blue background, snapdragons, gladiolus, dusty miller (artemisia) and chrysanthemums—in a range of color from pink to violet—duplicate the hues of dawn in an Eastern sky.

**GLORY TO GOD IN THE HIGHEST, PEACE TO MEN OF GOOD WILL;
FOR BEHOLD I BRING YOU TIDINGS OF GREAT JOY FOR ALL; FOR
THERE HAS BEEN BORN FOR YOU TODAY IN THE TOWN OF DAVID,
JESUS WHO IS THE SAVIOR, CHRIST THE LORD**

Luke 2:10, 11

CATHOLICISM

The Nativity

The rose has been a sacred flower since ancient times when
it was dedicated to chief mythological goddesses. Early Christians adapted pagan symbols that seemed appropriate with
their teachings and so the rose became a flower of the Virgin.
Here in the simple pattern of the "L" design wild roses stand
for promise. They combine with the weathered wood to make
a natural setting for the wonderful news of the coming of the
promised Messiah.

In color, spirituality and hope are expressed in the blue on
the figurine. This soft-toned blue, the rose of the flowers, the
green of the foliage, and gray of the wood are beautifully set
off against a rich royal-blue background.

**THEREFORE BEING JUSTIFIED BY FAITH, WE HAVE PEACE WITH GOD
THROUGH OUR LORD JESUS CHRIST**

Romans 5:1

PROTESTANTISM

Martin Luther

In the year 1517 Martin Luther wrote out on parchment his ideas of reform and nailed them to the door of the Church at Wittenberg—this is the subject of the painting which inspired the flower arrangement. Luther believed that the Church should be patterned after the Bible; this led him to give up many practices of the Roman Catholic Church. The Diet (Congress of the Empire) called Luther to trial at Worms, Germany, and ordered him to halt his teachings. He refused, and the reform spread. In 1529 the name "Protestant" was given to the movement.

Iris, juniper, geraniums, tuberoses, begonias, and a chrysanthemum are grouped into a vertical pattern, strengthened by the candle, the Light of the World. The vertical line is fitting interpretation because the courage and strength it symbolizes was inherent in the Reformation. The evergreen and the red and white of the flowers suggest immortality, courage, and truth.

II. Buddhism (page 22)

III. Protestantism (page 30)

IV. Judaism (page 28)

V. Catholicism (page 28)

REFORMATION

2

Themes from the
Life of Christ

In a book of interpretive religious themes, I have chosen the Redemptive story of Christianity as subject matter because from its earliest inception to the present day, people have fairly sung their way through the story of salvation; everywhere hymns of praise rise on the air.

It was in the beginning when the angel appeared unto Mary with the wonderful news that she was to be the Mother of Jesus, the Prince of Peace, that hymns of praise began with the song of her spirit, "My soul doth magnify the Lord." And at His birth the hymn, "Glory to God in the highest, peace on earth, good will toward men," was sung from the heavens by a choir of angels. Ever since, the Christian faith has been strengthened, the Church has been reassured, and the world made a better place in which to live, because man has kept alive in his heart the songs of faith, hope, peace, and love.

Christianity differs from all other religions for with it, God comes to man—*He* does the seeking; in other religious practices, man goes to God—*man* does the seeking. God gave us a covenant which He fulfilled with the gift of His Son in a manger. Writers of the four Gospels gave us a composite picture of Christ, the Son of God. Matthew presents Him as King of Israel; Mark depicts Him as the Suffering Servant; Luke portrays the human Christ; John records Him as the Word of God, the divine Son incarnated in human flesh—becoming like us that we may become like Him.

AND THOU SHALT CALL HIS NAME JESUS

Matthew 1:21

ANNUNCIATION

The lily as we know it today, like the rose, owes its introduction into Christian symbolism to pagan rites. A flower of the Virgin, its symbolism is steeped in spiritual significance. The Madonna lily which is seen here was not, it is generally agreed, native to Bible lands but the Old Masters painted it symbolically into their ecclesiastical art. From this the Madonna lily has become an especially popular symbol of Annunciation.

BEHOLD, I BRING YOU GOOD TIDINGS OF GREAT JOY

Luke 2:10

BIRTH OF JESUS

Just as the crescent of the moon borrows its light from the sun, so the Mother of Jesus borrows her glory from the Son of Righteousness. This crescent line so associated with our Lady of Peace sets the pattern for this design. The Madonna figurine is used in commemorating the birth of Jesus, for more than any other symbol it suggests the Christian joy of inward peace.

The lilies have significance since they are named for the Madonna; the evergreen symbolizes eternal life, the white of the carnations connotes purity, the grapes the "fruit of the womb," and the gold "throne" built up in a series of three, the Eternal Trinity.

IS NOT THIS THE CARPENTER'S SON?

Matthew 13:55

BOYHOOD

In relation to the figurine of the Boy Jesus, you will note the carpenter tools are overly large. Scale (proper size relationship) is a principle of art, but in this instance over size is justifiable. Here the tools are the key to the interpretation and must be prominent enough to serve as such in a forceful composition. Emphasis is on the vertical direction to characterize strength and courage. One branch of the weathered wood, in reverse swing to that of the geranium foliage on the opposite side, stretches outward, one reaches heavenward, the other earthward, symbolizing the unity of the human and divine in the Boy Jesus.

Geraniums, gladiolus, grass, dried magnolia blossoms, and fruits supply the plant material. A Biblical figurine and carpentry tools reveal the story suggested in the above Bible passage with obvious statement.

I MUST BE ABOUT MY FATHER'S BUSINESS

Luke 2:49

IN THE TEMPLE

The vertical line because it symbolizes strength and firmness is used here to suggest resolution and the awakening of the Messianic consciousness of divine purpose. The father and mother of Jesus upon their return to the Synagogue in search of the young boy were amazed at his knowledge and understanding. At this point, Mary must have remembered all those sayings she had kept in her heart, especially those referring to his mission as the promised Saviour of the world.

Hope and truth are symbolized by the gladiolus and white chrysanthemum; immortality by the green of the columbine foliage. Additional colors are the yellow of the gladiolus, the red of chemically treated bells of Ireland, and the blue of dyed daisies. The material is arranged in a gold antique vase on a marble-topped table. Texture and color were inspired by the Hoffman painting.

IF ANY MAN'S WORK ABIDE WHICH HE HATH BUILT THEREUPON, HE SHALL RECEIVE A REWARD

I Corinthians 3:14

JESUS, THE WORKER

The vertical design is very appropriate for this composition as it exemplifies strength, courage, and determination, characteristics of the Son of God.

The symbolism of flower is employed for its rich connotation with the church—especially the yellow roses associated with the promised Messiah. Biblical botanists have identified the anemone with which they are combined as one of the "lilies of the field" so plentiful along the way through which Jesus passed. Anemones live for us today not only in the good earth but in the ageless words from Luke 12:27: "Consider the lilies how they grow: they toil not, they spin not; and yet I say unto you, that Solomon in all his glory was not arrayed like one of these." The other materials arranged here are spoken of in the time of Jesus.

The base is an antique plaque carved with design of wine bottle and grapes. The figurine is white and gold.

THOU ART MY BELOVED SON

Mark 1:11

BAPTISM

Here is a composition with accent on the Biblical figurine
and the white dove to symbolize the spirit which descended
upon Jesus. Grapes and flowers flowing over the side of the
container suggest the fullness of the Spirit, or the overflowing
of the Spirit of God on His Beloved Son. Emphasis on white
speaks of joy, truth, and purity.

In a handmade Grecian compote, plant material includes
gladiolus, snapdragons, chrysanthemums and a "glamelia," a
flower composed of three gladiolus florets put together as one
bloom, beginning in the center with a bud, then larger petals
for the outer edge. All are wired on gladiolus stalk. A grace-
fully curved white base unites figure and arrangement.

THEY HAVE NO WINE

Gospel of John 2:3

FIRST MIRACLE

The symmetrical pattern used here in its formality and regal appearance is especially fitted for the occasion of a marriage feast, an event of great importance, and the setting for the first miracle Jesus performed. The empty wine bottle of red and clear glass helps to tell the story of His turning water into wine. The inclusion of grapes, fresh or artificial as in this composition, has significance since from them was made the wine with which Jesus symbolized his blood in the first communion.

Roses, carnations, snapdragons, chrysanthemums, and ivy and white, green, and violet plant material are used. Dark reddish leaves (galax) repeat the hue of the bottle pulling the arrangement and accessory into a harmonious whole.

I WILL MAKE YOU FISHERS OF MEN

Gospel of John 4:9

CALLS HIS DISCIPLES

The natural growth of the sea fan suggested that graceful curving line designated by the artist, William Hogarth, as the "line of beauty," and sets a pattern of simplicity for this composition. Commonplace materials are from both the sea and land. The container in the shape of a boat was inspired by the Bible passage above; it is placed on glass over green paper to simulate water. The figurine represents Peter, the first disciple called by Jesus.

Light pink to violet-red in this arrangement is striking against a sky-blue background.

BLESSED ARE THE PEACEMAKERS

Matthew 5:9

SERMON ON THE MOUNT

Calla lilies are the emblem of immortality—their whiteness the purity of truth. In symbolism they "march" here among serrated castor bean leaves and thorny red pods, their red hue and texture suggestive of the world's trials and tribulations.

The castor was one of the important leaves in Biblical times. It is arranged to suggest a tree which seems appropriate to the theme. In the Scripture trees were used figuratively. An example is found in Psalm 1:3: where a good and virtuous man is likened to "a tree planted by the rivers of water, that bringeth forth his fruit in his season; his leaf also shall not wither; and whatsoever he doeth shall prosper."

A restful mood is aided by the style of the arrangement, for placed as it is toward one end of the low rectangular container, a large area of its blue hue is exposed. And blue is the color of calmness. Water, an important part of this arrangement, symbolizes peace through the washing away of sin.

THIS DO IN REMEMBRANCE OF ME

Luke 22:19

THE LAST SUPPER

Asymmetry lends itself to this style of composition for it directs the eye easily to the accessory, an important and suggestive emblem in the interpretation. The red and green of the color plan, and the roses, carnations, and grapes have profound significance in the life and death of Jesus, and in the symbolism of the Church. Red, which is symbolic of passion and courage, takes on new meaning in the light of Jesus' words: "This is my blood which is shed for you." Ferns are appealing in the silhouette and in the language of plant material add their symbolism of sincerity.

HE IS RISEN; HE IS NOT HERE

Mark 16:6

THE RESURRECTION

At the time when Jesus walked on earth among men, his resurrection was a culmination of the past, present, and future life of the Christian Church. Without it our churches could not go forward, our faith could not be sustained—in fact, our civilization as we know it today could not exist.

To suggest this truth through arrangement, weathered wood is used to represent the past, fully blown magnolias and lilies the present, and flower buds the future. Christ is personified in the white figurine. To become significant through color the base of wood is gilded.

3

The Christmas Story

And the Angel said unto them, "Fear not! for, behold, I bring you good tidings of great joy, which shall be to all people. For unto you is born this day in the city of David a Saviour, which is Christ the Lord!

"And this shall be a sign unto you; ye shall find the babe wrapped in swaddling clothes, laying in a manger."

And suddenly there was with the Angel a multitude of the heavenly host praising God, and saying, "Glory to God in the highest, and on earth peace, good will toward men!" Luke 2:10-14

This ageless story makes Christmas unique and different from any other celebration in the world. It is a story of love, of peace, and of good will. When the "Wise Men" saw His star they had faith to act, to seek, to worship. We, at Christmas time, are moved to be like them for it seems that now, more than at any other time, we act upon our better impulses. We give of ourselves and of our substance, and in so doing, enrich our very lives. Once man experiences the real spirit of Christmas in his heart, his faith is increased, his zest for living is stimulated, and his life is broadened. It is with renewed confidence and hope that he reaches toward the future.

The anticipation which started when the Angel appeared to Mary still lives in the hearts of both young and old. We find it in the faith of a child, in the devotion of a mother, and in the compassion of our fellowmen.

WE HAVE SEEN HIS STAR . . . AND ARE COME TO WORSHIP HIM

Matthew 2:2

CHRISTMAS IS WORSHIP

It is fitting that a candle be an important feature in this interpretation, for through the centuries burning candles have honored Christ, the Light of the World.

On a styrofoam base, the vertical arrangement and painting make a symbolic asymmetrical triangle. The "Star of Jacob" is seen in the background. The star is associated also with Mary, the Mother of Jesus. With this emblem and crèche scene of the painting, and the candle we have the story of Christmas in visible form.

Color is a light blue in the background, red in the painting, gold in its frame, the star and candle, and white in the base and flowers. Huckleberry branches are treated with "sparkle dust."

Cedar could have just as well supplied the foliage for it is always good at Christmas. The Psalmist tells us that "Cedars also praise Him."

OH COME LET US SING UNTO THE LORD

Psalm 95:1

CHRISTMAS IS MUSIC

Music contributes to the observance of all Christmases as it did on that first Christmas when Christ was born. To symbolize the heavenly choir, beautiful ceramic angels delight the eye. Resplendent with "angel hair" (product of spun glass), a whitened branch, and Madonna figurine, we have an all white design of triangular shape on a tiered oblong base of styrofoam.

LET THE BEAUTY OF THE LORD OUR GOD BE UPON US

Psalm 90: 17

CHRISTMAS IS BEAUTY

The traditional red and green of Christmas are by-passed here for the newer plan of pink, gold, and white. The word "beauty" is exemplified in the bird, the vase, and the flowers. Rhythm in the dried heliconia leaves is accentuated by its repetition in the beautiful peacock accessory. Peacock and vase are antique gold leaf, the latter enriched with a swirling design of plant life in white.

The use of dried material, fully opened fresh bloom and buds symbolizes the past, present, and future to express the universal message of beauty in God's creation.

WHOSO SHALL GIVE A CUP OF COLD WATER IN MY NAME . . .

Matthew 10:42

CHRISTMAS IS SHARING

No plant material is more closely associated with Christmas than the holly and red poinsettia. And in particular they symbolize the desire to share that touches the heart of man during this joyous season. Legend tells us that the holly spreads kindness for it came into being where Jesus took his first baby steps, and the poinsettia (with the Christmas rose, ·Helleborus, and the white chrysanthemum) sprang from the ground to offer their beauty as gifts of love to the Christchild.

Flowers and foliage are arranged here in a crescent design, for in symbolism it ties together the Mother of Jesus who gave so much, and the Son who asked so little. The pitcher and the cup are realistic details· to complete the story.

INASMUCH AS YE HAVE DONE IT UNTO THE LEAST OF THESE MY BRETHREN . . .

Matthew 25:40

CHRISTMAS IS HOSPITALITY

Symmetrical design of formal balance gives dignity to this table set with refined appointments. The candles, the peacocks, and the white, gold, pink, and red colors tie in with the spiritual meaning of Christmas. Roses, carnations, snapdragons, Scotch and German heathers contribute their crisp freshness to delight the eye and set the stage for Christmas hospitality.

CHRISTMAS IS ANTICIPATION

With idea and accessories to please the child-like heart, this "L" design tells of a child's eager anticipation of Christmas morning. What little girl or boy—and indeed, adult—can resist the appeal of a Santa, his sleigh and reindeer? With carnations, balsam, and huckleberry foliage, a composition in traditional red, white, and green is presented against a green background.

HE THAT GIVETH LET HIM DO IT WITH LIBERALITY

Romans 12:8

CHRISTMAS IS GIVING

Here tulips of red in combination with the green pine are made more striking through contrast with white in the poinsettia at the main focal area. Those tulips which hang over the container are kept fresh in water-filled florist picks. These are wired to the pine branches in the center of the needle clusters. The Christmas packages are essential accessories; they contribute balance and theme continuity, and their wrappings repeat the red, green, and white in the arrangement—color so deeply intertwined in Christmas decoration. A bright red lamp base furnishes a harmonious container. Green at the background fits harmoniously into the plan.

FEAR NOT, FOR BEHOLD, I BRING YOU GOOD TIDINGS OF GREAT JOY . . .

Luke 2:10

CHRISTMAS IS JOY

The foliage of palm is appropriate in this interpretation for its radiating pattern suggests the radiance of joy. Feeling is strengthened in the poise of wonder assumed by the shepherd. He is in beige and brown which repeat color in the container. Hope, courage, truth, and joy are proclaimed by the red carnations and the white gladiolus and chrysanthemums.

FOR GOD SO LOVED THE WORLD THAT HE GAVE HIS ONLY BEGOTTEN SON

John 3:16

As a symbol of the promised Messiah the rose is included in this arrangement. For literally thousands of years this flower has held a place in religious symbolism for it was attributed to pagan goddesses of love. With Christianity, you will recall, its significance was transferred to the Virgin Mary.

Love is further symbolized by the secular emblem of cupid. The whitish edging of variegated holly unifies the white of the container with the green of the huckleberry, and the red of the berries, roses, and carnations.

4

The Fulfillment
of Easter

After Christ died on the cross and his body was placed in Joseph's burial cave, the disciples walked about in a daze; they were discouraged and disillusioned. Before Christ's death they felt secure in believing He was the promised Messiah. But when with divine power he did not lower Himself from the cross, doubt that He was the "Promised One" entered their hearts. Death had a finality about it that erased the exclamation point after the affirmation of their faith, and placed a period in its stead.

Later, however, when Jesus appeared alive to Mary Magdalene and others, hope began to revive. In subsequent appearances to the disciples, faith was completely restored. Christ was once again their Master and Lord. He had vanquished death and was alive forevermore. Their faith was the faith of an empty tomb; the faith of a living Christ; the faith of a joyous fellowship that warmed their hearts as they walked the ways of life.

For us today, faith exists as then—to bring us not to the memory of a dead Christ, but to the knowledge of a living Lord, our Redeemer. Easter and the everlasting joy of his resurrection renews in the Christian heart a surging faith in eternal life.

For this second great festival in the church year a profusion of flowers will carry out the triumph of Easter.

BLESSED ART THOU AMONG WOMEN, AND BLESSED IS THE FRUIT OF THY WOMB

Luke 1:42

MARY, THE MOTHER OF JESUS

The co-equality of the three Persons of the Holy Trinity: the Father, the Son, and the Holy Spirit is symbolized in the equilateral triangular shape of the arrangement. Interest is centered in the Madonna figurine with surrounding plant material suggestive of the role Mary was to play in the life and death of Jesus. Roses (promise) and carnations (purity) range in color from light pink to deep rose; an unidentified shrub gives line transition to space. The gray-green echeveria at the foot of the figure relates texture of plant material with that of the gray antique pewter compote.

IN HIM WAS LIFE; AND THE LIFE WAS THE LIGHT OF MEN

John 1:4

JESUS' MINISTRY

This horizontal arrangement with the lighted cross rising vertically at the center is representative of the divine nature of the Master. The cross and candle are reminder of the light and triumph of Jesus' ministry. Surrounding blooms of the magic lily (Lycoris squamigera) are suggestive of both life and sacrifice for the flower itself is a symbol of life, its orchid hue of sacrifice.

Other materials are common varieties of flowers—such as most likely grew by the wayside where Jesus ministered to the people. It is possible they were among the "lilies of the field" to which Jesus made reference when He preached to his disciples of worldly carefulness (Luke 12:27).

**YE SHALL FIND A COLT . . . BRING HIM HITHER. THE LORD HATH
NEED OF HIM**

Luke 19:30, 31

ENTRY INTO JERUSALEM

The date palm branches and daylily (Hemerocallis) were
selected because they are meaningful in the life of Jesus. The
Bible teaches that palm branches were strewn in His pathway,
while the lilies, beautiful for only one day, in symbolism represent the short-lived acclamation of the crowd on that day
when our Lord entered Jerusalem. The colt accessory is suggestive of the humility of Jesus. Yellow and green predominate.

The church commemorates this event in history as Palm
Sunday. Since it is not a festival day, restraint in decoration is
desired. It is interesting to follow tradition of heritage with
the use of palm as in this illustration made for a worship center
outside of the church. But branches of olive and sprouting
willow would be equally appropriate for the foundation of
the decorative unit, for these too are ancient Palm Sunday
custom.

**FATHER, IF THOU BE WILLING, REMOVE THIS CUP FROM ME:
NEVERTHELESS NOT MY WILL, BUT THINE, BE DONE**

Luke 22:42

GETHSEMANE

The weathered grapevine, the stone, and the brown base
suggest a garden scene; it was to the secluded retreat in the
Garden of Olives (Gethsemane) that Jesus prayed those words
that head this caption. The vine has further significance for
in a parable Jesus likened Himself to a vine, and his disciples
to its branches. The gladiolus is a symbol of hope. At the same
time its red hue, emphasized by contrast with green, is
reminder of His suffering. The blue cup in which the flowers
and foliage are arranged represents His humility; the figurine,
His supplication.

BUT JESUS SAID UNTO HIM, JUDAS, BETRAYEST THOU THE SON OF MAN WITH A KISS?

Luke 22:48

THE BETRAYAL

A muddy yellow or yellow modified with green has the connotation of treachery and deceit. In some Old Master paintings, the betraying Judas is clad in garments of this hue. To produce a morbid, brooding feeling of guilt in the arrangement, green-yellow in tulips, iris, statice, and chrysanthemums was chosen. Thirty pieces of silver at the base speak eloquently of Judas' treachery. The royal purple container represents the Kingship of Jesus.

I FIND IN HIM NO FAULT AT ALL

John 18:38

THE TRIAL

The scales of Christian symbolism are often shown out of balance to signify the unjust trial of Jesus. Here, the reverse is seen. The scales and arrangements in perfect balance suggest the perfect innocence of Jesus as pronounced three times by Pilate. The all-white twin arrangements consist of Easter lilies, snapdragons, stock, and gypsophila.

AND WHEN THEY WERE GONE TO THE PLACE WHICH IS CALLED CALVARY, THERE THEY CRUCIFIED HIM

Luke 23:33

THE CRUCIFIXION

The "crown of thorns" is made with the foliage of the spiny-toothed holly (Ilex cornuta) attached to a styrofoam wreath with red and white blooms of Japanese guava interwoven to signify both blood and water that flowed from the wounded Christ. Of the holly, legend says, the cruel crown was fashioned, with its white berries turning red, like drops of blood after the Crucifixion. The exotic and legendary Passion-flower* unites the crown and the styrofoam cross. The Mother of Jesus is personified by the kneeling figurine.

*Legend of the Passion-flower: The parts of a flowering vine found in the New World suggested the Passion of Christ to the early Spaniards, and thus the bloom became known as the Passion-flower. Close examination reveals these parts set forth by legend as follows:

ten petals—the apostles without Judas

circular corona—halo of Christ (some see in it the crown of thorns)

five anthers—five inflicted wounds

three stigmas—three piercing nails

tendrils—lashing whips

leaves—hands of the persecuters

HE IS NOT HERE, BUT IS RISEN

Luke 24:6

THE RESURRECTION

Mary, the Mother of Jesus, Mary Magdalene, and Salome were the first to hear of Jesus' resurrection. Bringing spices to the tomb, they found it empty except for the Angel clothed in shining garments of white who proclaimed, "He is not here, but is risen."

This interpretation is explicit with the angel and lilies, their resurrection message encompassing the "tomb" made of gray painted wood. So that the container would be subordinated, its hue matches that of the wood. The stone on the left gives transition softening the union of "tomb" and "ground," and weight for balance.

It is always of interest to think back on the cause of Christian symbolism and tradition. Why do we call the Sunday of the Resurrection Easter? And why is the lily that bears this same name traditionally used to glorify this glad day? Tradition of the Easter lily in celebration comes from the fact that the bloom is named for Eastre, a pagan goddess of spring for whom devotees of nature worship held a yearly festival. Early missionaries converted the Anglo-Saxon occasion in her honor to the Christian celebration of the Resurrection, maintaining the name of Eastre (Easter). Surely the acme of spring's message of life is reached with Easter and the lovely white flower that is the Easter lily.

5

Church Arrangements

The practice of placing a grouping of flowers in Temples began around the sixth century A.D. with the Chinese Buddhist priests. At first the offerings were very formal, gradually becoming less so as time went on.

History records that for centuries in the early Christian church flowers were not placed on the altar. Today, however, all over the world flowers are aranged for position on the altar where service is liturgical, and for other locations where worship follows more conservative ritual. The floral arrangements should be as carefully planned as the music rendered by the choir. Restraint should be a product of their design. Avoid the use of accessories for the problem of arranging flowers in the church differs from that of interpreting religious themes for home or public hall where the decoration tells a story in itself. In church it, like the music, is only a part of an allover effect; it complements and supplements the service, and even the sermon.

There is no restriction as to choice of plant material although some observances suggest an especially appropriate flower. A case in point is the festival of St. Michael. Where this is commemorated the Michaelmas daisy which bears his name would be a symbolic choice. But, in general, it is suitability in character that is paramount. A delicate arrangement of unsophisticated field daisies might be effective in a simple country church but it would be out of character in a high-vaulted cathedral. On the other hand, a heavy bold arrangement may be just the thing with heavy beams and tall spire-like features, but completely wrong in an edifice of less pretentious architecture and appointments.

To be sure the flowers will be visible to those in the rear of the congregation, choose large and distinct shapes. This is especially important if the church is large. If small blooms are used they can be made effective from a distance by massing. A variety in shape adds eye appeal. Spiked forms such as gladiolus or snapdragons give desirable height. Round shapes as the dahlia, or full forms as the iris or trumpet-shaped lily, give weight and stability to the design when they are used near the rim of the container. When only one type of bloom is available, foliage will supply variety. Choose it in harmonious color and texture and employ it to set off the flowers. If small-leaved foliage such as huckleberry is included as a filler, use quantities of it. Otherwise the green will be lost from the rear and the flowers then may stand out making the arrangement appear skimpy. At the same time, avoid overcrowding. The "ministry of flowers" should reflect a certain dignity and spirit of refinement; the overdone will not satisfy in this respect.

As to color, select hue in flowers as you would for any arrangement—that is, to harmonize or contrast with surroundings. Unless your church places restrictions in line with color designated for certain occasions, let the architecture of the building, the decor of the sanctuary, the lighting, the season of the year, and the location and space the arrangement will occupy guide you. It is advisable to consult a book dealing with the custom and tradition of your particular church.

When possible, use advancing hues (red and yellow), as retreating color (blue and many of the violet tones) fades under artificial lighting, or is lost in shadow or from a distance even in natural lighting. Light tone carries farther than dark. When light is dim, or when flowers are against a dark background, strong and bright color is best. A cheery red, for example, is dependable and harmonious when seen in relation to a gray stone interior, and yellow tones are pleasing with brown woodwork.

But you must keep in mind the color of the hangings and if the flowers will be in close proximity to them, supply a contrast in flower hue. At Pentecost, for instance, when it is customary to decorate with flowers of symbolic red, surround them with a contrast of white or green if the arrangement is against a red backdrop. Otherwise the flower color will melt into the background and be entirely lost to the congregation.

To study a book on the subject of liturgical color symbolism will be invaluable to you. I recommend Elizabeth Goldsmith's *Sacred Symbols in Art*. In general the approved color for major observances is as follows:

White is used prominently at Christmas, although red and green are popularly accepted as symbolic of the season. White is always proper too at Epiphany, Easter, Ascension, and Trinity Sunday.

In Reform synagogues the use of white flowers, symbol of purity and of being cleansed of sin, is very common on the Day of Atonement. White flowers are likewise used on the Festival of Shavuoth, the Feast of Weeks, on which Confirmation takes place. Here again the use of white symbolizes purity, innocence and other attributes usually associated with young people.

Green is prominent from Epiphany to pre-lent, and again after Trinity Sunday until Advent. The "green seasons" give opportunity for emphasis on shrub or tree branches to enrich worship. Not only is this material economical, but it offers a change from the usual, and variety in any experience is appreciated. In addition, their use is a custom of extreme antiquity. In Leviticus 23:40 we read: "And ye shall take you on the first day the boughs of goodly trees, branches of palm trees and boughs of thick trees, and willows of the brook; and ye shall rejoice before the Lord your God."

Red is assigned to *Pentecost* or *Whitsunday*. This is the third largest festival in the church year so keep this in mind as you decorate. There are few churches in which an arrangement with this hue dominant is not effective.

Violet is the color for solemn occasions, pre-Lent, and Lent with black on Good Friday and All Saint's Day when flowers are not used as a rule. Some churches are without flowers during the Advent season too.

The appropriate size of an arrangement is, of course, taken into account. The larger the space the flowers will occupy, the larger the arrangement and its component parts can be. And keep it high so it can be seen in the rear.

Eye level at which arrangements are viewed is a consideration. In denominational non-ritualistic churches flowers are placed on the communion table or the platform or pedestal near the pulpit. These will be seen at closer range than when the flowers are on the altar at the back of the chancel, and eye level becomes extremely important. If flowers are arranged at eye level and then moved to the position above, the arrangement may, and probably will, appear unbalanced. This would detract from rather than add to the impressiveness of the service.

Containers need not be expensive, but should be appropriate in character. Color, texture, line, and style are factors to be considered. In most cases bronze and brass are suitable, as also are alabaster, porcelain, and even pottery of high quality, so the choice is wide.

The actual design of the floral grouping is largely a matter of individual choice, although attention given to formal balance in the pattern with plant material high in the center of the vase graduating downward as it swings to the sides is desirable in most cases. And the aspiring design of a strong vertical is also a pleasing choice. Rising heavenward as in these designs seems especially fitting symbolism when we recall the Isaihan passage, "For as the heavens are higher than the earth, so are my ways higher than your ways, and my thoughts higher than your thoughts." (55:4)

There is, however, no valid reason why a more relaxed pattern cannot be satisfactory. It is the rule of *good taste* which must not be broken. Keep in mind that the arrangement must never distract in any way; it should without exception enhance the mood of worship. In churches of informal architecture the asymmetrically designed arrangement might be preferable, and there are instances in every church when it would even be desirable. There is, for example, the situation where two arrangements flank a cross. To arrange the plant material low on the side facing away from the cross and high toward it, will direct the eye to the arms of the cross pointing it up so to speak. Emphasized in this way the cross will dominate the setting as certainly is fitting this most important symbol of Christianity.

CHRISTMAS

White with its message of joy is especially appropriate, and therefore perhaps the most popular color for the altar on Christmas, the first great festival of the Church year. In this all-white arrangement interest is centered on the calla lilies, symbolic of immortality and typifying with their white and yellow all that man could hope for in the light of truth and goodness.

White caladium foliage with its magnificent pattern of green veining is transition to the decorative urn; gypsophila and snapdragon supply line interest and transition to space. In the interest of pleasing scale relationship the small flower shapes are massed into definable areas. To treat in this manner prevents the unpleasant effect of "too great difference in size" between them and the comparatively large lily forms.

EPIPHANY

(Twelfth Night)

Actually the origin of the celebration of the Epiphany (January sixth) is not certain, but a favored explanation claims that it celebrates the Magi's visit to the Christ Child. In some church calendars the Epiphany is celebrated the Sunday following January the sixth to commemorate the first manifestation of Christ to the Gentiles. With this latter in mind a white arrangement was composed. This seems appropriate for the sight of the whiteness moves one to recall through symbolic association with truth, the triumphant although delayed extension of the spirit of Christmas to the Gentiles.

LENT

The question is so often asked: Is it permissible to let plant material extend above the cross on the altar or communion table? No authoritative rule can be given in answer, although to keep it below the tip is a guard against subordinating the cross. The important consideration is that this emblem of the atoning death of our Savior stand free and dominate any flowers or candles nearby.

In this illustration flowers reach slightly higher than the cross, but they are arranged in a rhythmic sweep to direct the eye to it thus giving merited eminence. Although the arrangements are similar enough to appear as a pair, some variation in their designs prevents a static effect that is often presented in exact repetition.

Tones of violet are prominent here to symbolize penitence, humility, and sorrow. Violet snapdragons were chosen; daisies were sprayed with violet paint; copper-leaf foliage (Acalypha wilkesiana) was soaked in water for twenty-four hours in which time the leaves turned to a violet hue. Yellow daisies give contrast and tie in with the brass of the formal church containers. The sacred monogram, IHS, taken from early Christian abbreviation of Jesus' name in Greek, is clearly evident on the cross and vases.

EASTER

With expression of joy white contributes to our enjoyment of flowers in church on Easter Sunday. No flower is more suited than that which bears the significant name, Easter Lily; their trumpets seem to herald the fulfillment of the joyous day. Magnolias at the center of interest are a fitting companion for the noble lilies and add variety of form; their lovely golden-brown stamens blend perfectly with the bronze of the container. Yellow in the throat of the lilies repeats the tone of brass in its base and handles, and their shapes repeat its rhythmic lines to result in a beautiful and harmonious composition.

PENTECOST

(Whitsunday)

On Pentecost the world received the gift of the Christian church. To commemorate the descent of the Holy Spirit upon the Apostles, Christians celebrate this festival on the seventh Sunday after Easter. Scripture teaches that fire was a manifestation of the Holy Spirit so red to signify fire is the predominating color in this arrangement. A contrast of green enriches it. Emphasis on red conveys other symbolism too, for it represents the great sacrifice achieved for all. It is reminder that man can rejoice in God's Holy Comfort.

In the copper-washed vase, dracaena leaves almost matching in hue are included to harmonize container and plant material.

THANKSGIVING

Through the ages the harvest has been a season for rejoicing. Here a bronze urn holds plant material in complementary colors of yellow and violet arranged in oval design to depict the fullness and bounty of God's goodness to us. In addition it represents four periods in the cycle of plant life—and for that matter, our own!—planting, growing, harvesting, using. The spring tulips, the summer gladiolus, the autumn chrysanthemum, and the winter statice are remainder of God's ever-present care.

Even though it is America's "Pilgrim Day" that is celebrated as a time of special thanksgiving in this country, many churches in Virginia follow England's tradition with actual crops carried into the church. English settlers in this part of the New World, unlike those who landed at Plymouth Rock, didn't hope to gain religious freedom; they retained many customs of their homeland.

It is always appropriate for the church's ceremony of Thanksgiving to use fruits and/or vegetables and/or grains in decoration, for it is on the "fruits of the earth" that man's physical well-being depends, and God intends that man be physically as well as spiritually whole. Just a simple grouping of wheat, the staff of life, standing upright with grape clusters, symbol of abundance, at the base can give suitable dignity, and eye appeal as well.

VII. Christmas is hospitality (page 56)

VIII. *He causeth the grass to grow*
(page 84)

IX. *The Lord God planted a garden* (page 82)

XI. *Behold, how great a matter a little fire
kindleth* (page 86)

X. *A Sanctuary* (page 83)

6

Our Heritage

A Conservation Series

  "And God said, Behold I have given you every herb bearing seed . . . and every tree . . . and every green herb." Genesis 1:29. Surely man should respect these gifts God has so generously entrusted to our keeping. In fact the Bible urges mankind to protect and use wisely the natural resources. For this reason a conservation series is included in this book dealing with religious themes. It is planned especially for program material among organized groups. In the knowledge that conservation is every one's work, programs intended to impress individuals with their duty and privilege in protecting and using our wonderful heritage in the proper way, must be interestingly presented. With this thought in mind, interpretive arrangement is a new approach to our conservation problem with education and life enrichment as well as beauty becoming beneficial factors. It is with reverence that I presume to use the Scriptures for this purpose.

Following the arrangements in the conservation series, a heritage from psalm and prayer is described and interpreted.

AND THE LORD GOD PLANTED A GARDEN . . .

Genesis 2:8

A GARDEN OF BEAUTY

Against a contrasting light blue blackground, bright warm hues of yellow-orange, orange-yellow and orange-red in fruit and flower with pine form a triangular arrangement. Interest is centered in the painted waterfall. The combination creates a natural "garden of beauty" with color, fruit, and pine adding symbolize association. Other materials include tithonia, yarrow, celosia and tuberous begonia.

BY THEM SHALL THE FOWLS OF THE HEAVEN HAVE THEIR HABITATION, WHICH SING AMONG THE BRANCHES . . .

Psalm 104:12

A SANCTUARY FOR WILDLIFE

Arranged within the freedom of an asymmetrical triangle, birds are positioned here in a sanctuary of maple foliage, chrysanthemums, ageratum, goldenrod, stones, and cypress wood. We are reminded that God provides even for the wildlife of the forest. The "ground" is insulation board. Sky-blue is appropriate background color and pleasing foil for the flower hues.

HE CAUSETH THE GRASS TO GROW . . . THE HERB FOR THE SERVICE OF MAN; THAT HE MAY BRING FORTH FOOD OUT OF THE NIGHT

Psalm 104:14

PLENTY

On a hand-carved Early American table, brown containers hold red-violet beautyberry from a native shrub (Callicarpa), pink spirea and chrysanthemums, yellow spoon chrysanthemums, and yellow roses to spill over the edge of the shelves. A variety of fruit contributes symbolism. And on the lowest level a symbolic cornucopia also adds to the theme of *plenty* in this triple arrangement to reveal the bounty and richness of the earth.

BEHOLD, HOW GREAT A MATTER A LITTLE FIRE KINDLETH!

James 3:5

DESTRUCTION

Destruction is the inspiration behind this interpretation. On a black base is charred wood "flaming" with red carnations and gladiolus. Red geranium "sparks" spread the fire upward and forward along the fast moving diagonal line supplied by dried black branches. Placement of the bird suggests a flight to safety and increases emotional response in the viewer.

A FIRE DEVOURETH BEFORE THEM; . . . BEHIND THEM A DESOLATE WILDERNESS

Joel 2:3

DESOLATION

On a black base, a minimum of palmetto and magnolia foliage burnt to blackness suggest desolation left by fire—a fire caused, perhaps, by human carelessness. The pattern set by a heaven, man and earth line in the manner of Japanese arrangement was chosen as reminder of man's relation in the universe.

THE WATERS WEAR THE STONES: THOU WASHEST AWAY THE THINGS WHICH GROW OUT OF THE DUST OF THE EARTH; AND THOU DESTROYEST THE HOPE OF MAN

Job 14:19

EROSION

On a base of sand grooved to give the impression of soil erosion, the evergreen, symbol of eternal life, emblemizes here the struggling but triumphant growth of a tree as it pushes its roots deeply into the ground for needed moisture and food. The simile is that man, even from a shriveled soul, can grow spiritually when he digs his roots deeply into Christ-like living. Too many dwell in barren soil when the water of life is theirs for the asking.

Grasses, echeveria, and dried foliage supply other appropriate texture and form.

THUS SAYEST THE LORD; I WILL TAKE A BRANCH OF THE HIGHEST CEDAR, AND WILL SET IT; I WILL CROP OFF FROM THE TOP OF HIS YOUNG TWIGS . . . AND WILL PLANT IT

Ezekiel 17:22

RESTORATION

Emphasis on the vertical direction shows the results of good cultivation as suggested here. Strong texture and form, and clear color throughout the composition are likened to the dividends of skillful planning and planting. The tools tie in with the theme of *restoration,* and are junctional elements between the smaller greens in readiness for transplanting into the ground and the flowers and foliage already restored to vigorous growth.

The Twenty-third Psalm

Added to natural resources numerous sacred writings record man's heritage. I have chosen the Twenty-third Psalm* as a favorite for it is so full of meaning for me. As a small child I memorized the words, and I say "words" advisedly for they were to me then mere words. But as I grew older they began to live, becoming words of meaning and faith.

*The Lord is my shepherd; I shall not want.

He maketh me to lie down in green pastures; he leadeth me beside the still waters.

He restoreth my soul; He leadeth me in the paths of righteousness for His name's sake.

Yea, though I walk through the valley of the shadow of death,

I will feel no evil; for thou art with me; thy rod and thy staff they comfort me.

Thou preparest a table before me in the presence of mine enemies; thou anointest my head with oil; my cup runneth over.

Surely goodness and mercy shall follow me all the days of my life: and I will dwell in the house of the Lord for ever.

My first great test came when at the age of twelve, I walked through the forest, alone and afraid. When panic was at its peak, the "still small voice" came, and "The Lord is my Shepherd" was a living reality. I reached out my hand and placed it in His just as I would like to have reached for my earthly father's hand had he been near. It was then that I heard the singing of the birds, that I saw the beauty of the trees, and I knew I was a part of it all.

As time went on "Even though I walk through the shadow of death I will fear no evil" became a bright and shining light. At my lowest moment, when there was no physical evidence that I would live, I felt His hand and knew I was not to die. "For my Shepherd took me by the hand and led me to a fairer land." This is a land, not of a future world, but a land of here and now. A land in which I can help to cultivate a garden of God where goodness, truth, and beauty grow.

The following eight arrangements draw inspiration from this Psalm. The quoted lines furnish subject matter for the descriptive comments.

THE LORD IS MY SHEPHERD

The past, the present, and the future are conveyed here with weathered wood, fully opened bloom, and buds. With no beginning and no ending the circle interprets our subject, for the Great Shepherd was, is, ever will be in our hearts; there is no beginning or ending to God.

White, the essence of all colors is presented in the flowers with the beautiful white Calla lily a symbol of immortality; gold which speaks of purity and divine light, in the styrofoam circle and base.

HE MAKETH ME TO LIE DOWN IN GREEN PASTURES

Design: Horizontal—no line could be more appropriate for the structure of this composition, for the attributes of tranquility and repose in the horizontal are especially suited to interpret this inspiring line from the Twenty-third Psalm.

Someone has said, "Let him bear the palm that merits it," so palm is included to symbolize reward of victory of oneself. White with its impression of truth predominates in the plant material.

HE RESTORETH MY SOUL

In the oriental manner of heaven, man, and earth construction, pussy willows were gently bent after having been cut in groups of three.

With their gray furry catkins emerging from their shiny brown shells the pussy willows declare that winter has made way for spring. The tulips lift their chalice cups to be filled with warmth and gladness. Human personality needs the "Son" of gladness to restore, to make new, to put joy and singing back into the hearts of man.

THY ROD AND THY STAFF THEY COMFORT ME

To symbolize courage, spirituality, and nobility, purple (a mixture of red and blue) dominates this plan; the golden staff represents that of the shepherd. The thought this stimulates in the mind is that just as the shepherd leans upon his staff with patience and kindness as he tends his sheep, so the shepherd of our lives watches and protects the human flock in times of need. To carry symbolism further all is confined within the boundary of a symmetrical triangle.

THOU ANOINTEST MY HEAD WITH OIL

This is a spiritual theme of supplication for grace to be bestowed upon those who serve their fellow men.

The blue of the fabric and the golden arch are used to signify penitence. The white of gladiolus bloom symbolizes purification, and the lily the restoration of one who is being anointed.

MY CUP RUNNETH OVER

Why are flowers arranged here to seemingly overflow the cup in which they are grouped? Because such design represents the overflowing of abundance—how rich and abundant our blessings!

Yellow predominates in this cup of happiness which is spilling over with pure joy, for yellow is emblematic of the sun, the essence of physical light and glory.

Materials include gladiolus, snapdragons, lily foliage, acacia, calendulas, ranunculus, and a chrysanthemum in a green glass cup and a black velvet background.

XII. *So then faith cometh by hearing* (page 104)

SURELY GOODNESS AND MERCY SHALL FOLLOW ME

Seven variously colored candles in a brass candelabrum dominate this composition. At the center a candle of white represents the Great Shepherd. The other hues are blue for spirituality and hope, red for courage and strength, yellow for joy and happiness, orange for warmth and gladness, green for faith and immortality, purple for royalty. In the light of this symbolism, let us examine our own lives. If we practice the principles for which these hues stand, we will leave behind us a beauty like the afterglow of an Arizona sunset. Flowers grouped to follow the line of beauty of the weathered wood create an appropriate accessory because the beauty of its curve suggests a combination of grace and joy inherent in that individual who practices love and justice in his daily life.

AND I SHALL DWELL IN THE HOUSE OF THE LORD FOREVER

The diagonal line on which this composition is based gives movement upward as well as forward, hence the pattern selected to interpret *ascending of the spirit*. Airy materials heighten the theme.

Against a background of symbolic blue, sago palm, huckleberry (painted off-white), artificial white heather, royal blue Christmas tree balls, and gilded styrofoam base and cross present a composition in white, gold, green, and blue.

The Prayer of St. Francis

From among other favorite writings I include the beautiful and thought provoking prayer assigned to St. Francis of Assisi, patron of creatures in the wild. This humble servant renounced wealth to go into the fields and forests for his temporal and spiritual blessings. His prayer gives to the world a code to live by, so has a definite place in a Chapter on *"Our Heritage."*

> *Lord, make me an instrument of Thy peace:
> Where there is hatred, let me sow love;
> Where there is injury, pardon;
> Where there is doubt, faith;
> Where there is despair, hope;
> Where there is darkness, light;
> And where there is sadness, joy.
> Oh Divine Master, grant that I may not seek
> To be consoled, as to console;
> To be understood, as to understand;
> To be loved, as to love;
> For it is in giving that we receive;
> It is in pardoning, that we are pardoned; and
> It is in dying that we are born to eternal life.

Verses from the Bible serve as headings for the following interpretive arrangements, for surely such was the source of thought and living for St. Francis of Assisi, and the inspiration for the stirring prayer.

**HOW BEAUTIFUL UPON THE MOUNTAINS ARE THE FEET OF HIM
THAT PUBLISHETH PEACE**

Isaiah 52:7

In this triangular composition interest is centered in the
white dove, the symbol of peace. Peace roses have been included because of name association.

Green and white snow-on-the-mountain, spiney blue-green
juniper, and beige-colored weathered wood complete the design constructed on a free-form base of matching hue.

LOVE YOUR ENEMIES . . . DO GOOD TO THEM THAT HATE YOU

Matthew 5:44

A grouping of roses, the Queen of Heaven to the early Christians, designs this interpretation. Let it be remembered that the rose was also the flower of Venus, the pagan goddess of love and beauty. And Cupid, a *secular* love emblem, carries the mass of dark red roses (Eventide) to express *divine* love through their hue.

SO THEN FAITH COMETH BY HEARING, AND HEARING BY THE WORD OF GOD

Romans 10:17

Since white expresses innocence, white roses, gladiolus, and artificial grapes are used here to symbolize the *receiver* of faith, and the gladiolus the *giver* of faith through nobility attached to their purple hue. To symbolize a "reaching up with courage and strength," a vertical pattern is employed. An open Bible reveals the word: If ye have faith as a grain of mustard seed . . ."

WHICH HOPE WE HAVE AS AN ANCHOR OF THE SOUL

Hebrews 6:19

Since early Christian days the anchor has been the ecclesiastical symbol of hope—promise for the future which strengthens man's soul. You see it here dominating a design built on a crescent line which Christianity associates with the Mother of Jesus, from whence comes man's hope of immortality.

LET YOUR LIGHT SO SHINE

Matthews 5:16

In the Holy Bible, God, Christ, truth, and virtue are identified with light, and the Devil and wrong-doing with darkness. In this arrangement strong contrast of white and black
is vivid and forceful to symbolize light as opposed to darkness.
With lighted candle, a traditional symbol, and luminous white
hydrangeas, the design clearly interprets the desire of St. Francis to show light where there is darkness.

OH LET THE NATIONS BE GLAD AND SING FOR JOY

Psalm 67:4

In this composition the smoked glass epergne suggests the cloud that sometimes overshadows mankind with sadness. But we see that sadness is overpowered by happiness, for the arrangement's dominant hue is yellow, emblematic of the sun. Then too, flowers and foliage radiate from the heart of the design in circular pattern expressing joy and completeness. Is this not the goal for the brotherhood of man in all nations?

Plant materials are goldenrod, the Queen of the meadow, chrysanthemums, roses, and foliage of the August lily (hosta).

7

Reference Lists

The sacred, secular, and psychological association of plants and parts of plants, objects, and elements of design presented here are compiled from extensive research, but for a more complete list and more detailed treatment than space allows in this manual, I refer you to books to be found in almost any good public library. The *how* and *why* these and other symbols come to produce a common thought in the minds of men is fascinating reading. The following titles are particularly helpful:

Flower lore, and Mythological:

MYTHS AND LEGENDS OF FLOWERS, TREES, FRUITS, AND PLANTS
—*Charles M. Skinner*

FLORA'S INTERPRETER—*Hale*

THE FLORAL SYMBOLISM OF THE GREAT MASTERS—*C. Welsh*

Pagan and Early Christian:

A HANDBOOK OF ORNAMENT—*Franz Sales Mayer*

CEREMONIES OF THE ROMAN RITE—*Fortescue*

ARCHITECTURE AND SETTING OF THE ANGLICAN WORSHIP—
Addeshaw and Etchells

Psychological:

GIVING AND GETTING AWARDS IN FLOWER ARRANGEMENT—
Emma Hodkinson Cyphers

Symbolism of Flowers, Leaves, and Fruits
Almond, flowering ("wake tree") —spring; hope
Amaranth—immortality
Anemone—anticipation
Apple—temptation
Azalea—temperance
Bamboo—strength
Chrysanthemum—autumn (Chinese)
Clover—the Trinity
Cock—Passion dawn
Columbine—gifts of the spirit
Crocus—cheerfulness
Crown Imperial—majesty
Crown of thorns (passion)
Daisy (white) —innocence
Dianthus (pink) —Divine love
Elder—compassion
Evergreen—eternal life
Fern—sincerity
Fig—fruitfulness
Fleur-de-lis—Virgin
Gladiolus—hope
Goldenrod—encouragement
Grape—Holy Communion; abundance (Wild) —charity
Grapes plus Wheat—Holy Eucharist
Grass (any variety) —submission
Hawthorne—hope
Heather—loneliness
Hyacinth (violet) —sorrow
Iris—The Virgin Mary; majesty; power
Ivy—longevity; everlasting life
Jasmine—grace; elegance
Laurel—glory; atonement
Lilac (white) —modesty
Lily, Calla—immortality; modesty
Lily, Easter—life; resurrection
Lily, Madonna—immortality; resurrection; chastity; purity
Lily of the valley—purity
Lotus—immortality; service; summer (Chinese)
Myrtle—immortality; generosity; peace
Narcissus—good fortune
Oak—power; strength
Olive branch—peace
Orchid—love; beauty; nobility
Palm leaves—eternal peace; victory
Passion-flower—Passion of the Lord; belief
Peony—high position in China; spring (Chinese)
Pine—immortality; winter

Pineapple—hospitality
Plum (white) —winter (Chinese)
Pomegranate—resurrection; fertility; abundance
Poppy (red) —consolation
Potato—benevolence
Pussy willow—spring
Quince—temptation
Rose—promised Messiah; Madonna; Love (divine and secular)
  Single—simplicity
Rudbeckia—justice
Snowdrop—hope
Strawberry—Virgin
Sycamore—Virgin
Turnip—generosity
Violet—humility; modesty
  (White) —innocence
Vine (grape) —Christ
Water lily—silence; regeneration
Water—purification
Wheat—staff of life

Secular, Mythological, and Early Christian Symbols
Anchor—hope
Arch (pointed) —aspiration; growth
Bread—The Lord's broken body
Butterfly—the Resurrection
Candle—Light of the World
Candelabrum (seven branched) —Judaism; seven gifts of the
  spirit
  Two branched (or two candles) —the Lord's two-fold nature
    (human and divine)
Circle—God's eternal existence
Cornucopia—abundance
Crosier staff—authority
Cross Latin—Christianity
  green—tree of life
  red—blood of Christ
  gold—glory
Cross (Christian) —Christ; sacrifice; triumph
Crown of thorns—Christ's suffering
Cup—Gethsemane
Cupid—love
Dove—peace
  (descending) —Holy Spirit; baptism
Dragon—Satan; evil
Eagle—St. John, evangelist
Fish—Secret sign, Lord's Supper; miracle
Fishermen—Baptism

Frankincense (fragrant resin for incense) —holiness
Griffen (union of lion's body and eagle's head and wings) —fire
Halo—divine light
Heart—charity
Helmet—salvation
IHS—monogram of Jesus
Incense—holiness
Lamp—Word of God
Lion (quiet poise) —Redeemer
   (roaring) —devil
Lyre—Concord
Moon—Crescent—Virgin
Myrrh (fragrant gum for incense) —suffering
Nails—Christ's suffering
Peacock—resurrection
Phoenix—resurrection
Pillar and cord—scourging
Pomegranate—royalty (bursting) resurrection
Ram's horn—Jewish New Year
Scales (unbalanced) —unjust trial of Jesus
   (balanced) —justice
Serpent—sin; wickedness; temptation
Shamrock—trinity; St. Patrick
Shepherd—Christ
Scroll—Wisdom; attributes of Apostles
Shield—faith
   (with crescent moon) —glory of the Virgin Mary
   (with 'lily) —the Annunciation
   (with rose) —promise of the Messiah
Staff—refuge; strength
Star—divine light
   (five pointed) —Virgin Mary
   (six pointed) —star of David
Ship—salvation
Sun—happiness
Sword—Holy Spirit
Torah—Jewish Law
Triangle (equilateral) —Trinity
Units of three—Trinity
Wine—Christ's shed blood
Wreath—eternity— (fruit, flowers) cycle of seasons

Symbolism of Color (Sacred and Psychological)
Yellow (bright, warm) —happiness; sun; warmth
   (muddy, cool green-yellow) —cowardice; deception; jealousy
Red—courage; aggressiveness; martyrdom; love; warmth
Blue—spirituality; serenity; hope; coolness

Orange—warmth; gladness; activity
Green—faith; hope; life; immortality
Purple (deep) —leadership; royalty; nobility
Vine—Christ
Violet (light, orchid) —sacrifice; penitence; sorrow; shadow
White—purity; innocence; goodness; joy; truth
Gray—softness; insecurity; hope
Black—despair; evil; death
Gold—purity; divine light
Values:
  Dark—mystery; quiet; dignity
  Light—gayness; ethereal quality
Intensity:
  Bright—pompousness
  Grayed—simplicity; hope

Symbolism of Line and Shape (Sacred and Psychological)
    Line
Curve
  concave—hardship; emptiness
  convex—fullness; maturity
  crescent (of new moon) —Glory of the Virgin Mary
  deep—exuberance; abundance
  shallow—grace; tenderness
  parabolic (New. Used with vertical) —power
  spiral—mystery; complexity; expectancy
Straight
  diagonal—action; danger; uncertainty; insecurity
  horizontal—repose; calm; security
  radiating—happiness; excitement
  vertical—aspiration; nobility; faith; strength; stability; vigor;
    courage
  zigzag—disquiet; confusion
    Shape or Form
Circle—continuity; completeness; maturity; fulfillment;
    eternity
Fan—happiness
Oval—continuity; completeness
Pyramid—strength; composure
Rectangle—strength; dependability
Square—strength; dependability
Triangle (equilateral) —Trinity
  (Japanese asymmetrical) —Union of man with nature

It has taken two hundred years or more to identify the
thousands of references made to plants in the pages of the
Bible. It is said that some plants are now extinct, others differ
in appearance to those known in Bible days, and still others
are given modern names. For example, the "rose of sharon"

is the flower we know today as the *tulip;* the "sword lily" is our gladiolus. Some names are of a general order. Corn, for instance, alludes to various grains and does not refer to maize or Indian corn, for this plant was unknown in Bible times. Although there was the Chalcedonicum lily and a rose similar to a type known today, botanists believe "lily" and "rose" are general Scriptural terms including a variety of flowers. When Isaiah tells us "The desert shall blossom as the rose" or Hosea, "Israel . . . shall grow as the lily," we must not confuse these with the rose and lily of our modern gardens.

As with the symbols, to list all the plants of the Bible would fill a large volume; only a partial listing is attempted and there is room for only one Bible source. Actually, reference to most of the named plants is found more than once through the pages of the Bible, while others are met over and over again. A must for reading if you wish to fill out the sketchy record supplied below is *The Plants of the Bible* by Dr. Harold Moldenke.

Some Flowers, Foliage, and Fruits of the Bible:
Aloes—John 19:39
Anise (dill) —Matthew 23:23
Apple (golden), apricot, quince, citron—Joel 1:12
Aspalathus—Ecclesiastes 24:15
Barley (Biblican corn) —Exodus 9:31
Bean—II Samuel 17:27
Bitter herb—Numbers 9:9
Bramble—Judges 9:8
Bulrush (papyrus) —Exodus 1:22
Burning bush (crimson-flowered mistletoe) —Exodus 3:1
Camphire—Solomon 4:13
Cockle—Job 31:38
Cotton—Esther 1:5
Cucumber—Isaiah 1:8
Cumin—Isaiah 28:26
Fig—Revelation 6:13
Fitches—Isaiah 28:25
Flax—Exodus 30:34
Frankincense (an herb which grows like a tree) —Matthew 2:10
Herb (green things—not small plants of our herb garden) —
     Genesis 1:11
Galbanum—Exodus 30:34
Gall (wild gourd) —Matthew 27:32
Garlic—Numbers 11:5
Gourd (castor bean) —Jonah 4:6
Grape—Numbers 13:23
Grass (a variety) —Luke 12:28

Hyssop—John 19:28
Ivy—Maccabees 6:6
Leek—Numbers 11:1
Lentil—Genesis 25:29
Lily (Chalcedonicum), turk's cap—Solomon 51:13
lily (Iris)—Ecclesiastes 50:80
Lily of the field (Anemone and others)—Luke 12:27
Mallow—Job 30:4
Mandrake—Genesis 30:14
Melon (watermelon)—Numbers 11:4
Mint—Luke 11:42
Mustard (herb which grows to tree height)—Matthew 13:31
Myrrh— (a fragrant gum from herb of tree height)—Matthew
    2:11
Narcissus—Isaiah 35:1
Oleander—Ecclesiiastes 39:13
Onion—Numbers 11:5
Onycha—Exodus 30:34
Pomegranate—I Samuel 14:2
Reed (cattail; sorghum)—Job 40:15
Rie—Exodus
Rolling thing (Christian immortality)—Isaiah 17:13
Rose of Sharon (tulip)—Solomon 2:1
Rue—Luke 11:42
Rush—Job 8:9
Saffron (crocus)—Solomon 4:13
Scarlet—Leviticus 14:48
Spikenard (Aralia)—Mark 14:3
Star of Bethlehem—II Kings 6:25
Statice—Exodus 30:34
Sugar cane—Isaiah 43:23
Tare (weed)—Matthew 13:25
Thistle—Genesis 3:17
Thorn, Crown of (Jerusalem thorn)—Mark 15:17
Vine, grape—Micah 4:3
Vine of Sodom—Deuteronomy 32:32
Water lily—I Kings 7:19
Wheat (Biblican corn)—Genesis 41:4
Wild gourd (gall)—II Kings 4:39
Wormwood—Revelations 8:10

Some Trees and Shrubs of the Bible
Algum—II Chronicles 2:3
Almond—Numbers 17:1
Alning—I Kings 10:1
Aloes—Psalm 45:7
Apple—Proverbs 25:11
Balm—Ezekiel 27:17

Box—Isaiah 41:10
Carob—Luke 15:16
Cassia—Exodus 30:32
Cedar—Numbers 19:1
Cedar of Lebanon—Ezekiel 31:8
Cinnamon—Revelation 18:13
Cypress—Isaiah 44:13
Desire—Ecclesiastes 12:5
Ebony—Ezekiel 27:15
Fig—Isaiah 60:13
Frankincense (resin burned as incense from the Sycamore) —
    Matthew 2:10
Goodly fruit—Leviticus 23:39
Green bay tree—Psalm 37:35
Hemlock—Hosea 10:2
Judas tree—Matthew 27:3
Juniper (desert broom) —I King 19:3
Locust—Matthew 3:1
Myrrh (fragrant gum from herb which grew to tree height) —
    Matthew 2:11
Myrtle (shrub reaching tree proportions) —Zechariah 1:7
Oak (Holly) —Genesis 35:6
  (Valonia) —Zechariah 11:1
Oil tree—Isaiah 41:18
Olive—Genesis 8:6
Oriental plane—Genesis 30:37
Palm (date) —Numbers 33:9
Pine—I Samuel 14:2
Poplar—Genesis 30:37
Shittah (Acacia) —Isaiah 41:13
Sycamine—Luke 17:5
Sycamore (its dried gum is called "frankincense) —Amos 7:14
Tamarix—Samuel 18:33
Turpentine—Ecclesiastes 24:16
Walnut—Solomon 6:10
Weeping willow (Aspen) —Psalm 137:1
Willow—Isaiah 44:1

Suggested Flower Show Schedules

1. GREAT RELIGIONS OF THE WORLD

I. JUDAISM
1. Hanukkah—"Festival of Lights."
2. Chavuoth—Anniversary of the Ten Commandments.
3. Passover—Celebration of Hebrew liberation from bondage.
4. Yom Kippur—Jewish New Year.
5. Succoth—Feast of Tabernacles.

II. BUDDHISM
1. Buddha—The Enlightened One.
2. Purity and Perfection—Wheel of the Law.
3. Buddhist Monks—Example of the Way of Life.
4. Tokonoma—Alcove in Japanese home with flower arrangement.
5. Rikka—Standing flowers. First temple arrangement.

III. HINDUISM
1. The God Siva; symbol of creation and destruction.
2. Animals. Reverence. Transmigration.
3. Benares. Sacred Hindu city on banks of Ganges River.
4. Karma. Final salvation attained by good record.
5. Ancestral Worship.

IV. MOHAMMEDANISM
1. One God: Allah.
2. Prayer. Five times daily facing Mecca.
3. Almsgiving. Offering to Allah.
4. The Feast of Ramadan.
5. Pilgrimage to Mecca.

V. CATHOLICISM
1. The Nativity. "Glory to God in the highest."
   Luke 2:14
2. The Church. "Thou art Peter; and upon this rock."
   St. Matthew 16:16
3. The Holy Eucharist. "Jesus took bread and blessed it."
   Luke 24:30
4. The Crucifixion. "And I, if I be lifted up . . ."
   St. John 12:32
5. The Resurrection. "Christ has risen as He said."
5. The Resurrection. "He is not here; for He is risen."
   St. Matthew 28:6

116

VI. PROTESTANTISM
    1. Birth of Jesus
    2. Resurrection
    3. Salvation by faith alone
    4. Priesthood of the believer
    5. Martin Luther

2. THE PSALMS

I. Psalm I
    1. "Blessed is the man . . ."
    2. "He shall be like a tree . . ."
    3. "He delights in the law of the Lord."
    4. "He shall prosper . . ."
    5. "He shall meditate . . ."

II. Psalm 23
    1. "The Lord is my Shepherd"
    2. "He leadeth me beside still waters"
    3. "He restoreth my soul . . ."
    4. "Thy rod and thy staff they comfort me"
    5. "My cup runneth over"

III. Psalm 27
    1. "The Lord is my light . . ." (to include a candle)
    2. "To behold the beauty of His temple . . ." (An arrangement for the Altar)
    3. "I will sing praises unto the Lord . . ." (Interpretation of a hymn. A verse to accompany exhibit)
    4. "I had fainted, unless I had believed" (A composition to interpret Faith)
    5. "Wait on the Lord . . ." (A composition to interpret a quiet mood)

3. THE LIFE AND MINISTRY OF JESUS

I. The Sayings of Jesus—the saying to accompany exhibit
Example: "I am the vine, ye are the branches."

II. The Parables of Jesus—the parable to accompany exhibit
Example: "The kingdom of heaven is like unto a man who sowed good seed."

III. The Death of Jesus. A composition to interpret this or any event in the week preceding the Crucifixion.
Example: "And when they were come to Calvary . . . there they crucified Him."
(Name the event)

IV. The Resurrection of Jesus. A composition to interpret the triumph of Easter Sunday

4. HYMNS OF THE CHURCH

Title, line, or verse must accompany exhibit
1. God
   Example: "Holy, Holy, Holy."
2. The Church
   Example: "I love Thy kingdom Lord."
3. The Fellowship
   Example: "Blest be the Tie that Binds."
4. Worship
   Example: "O Worship the King."
5. Service
   Example: "Are ye able said the Master."

5. CROSSES OF THE WORLD
1. Christian Crosses
   Example: Latin Cross
2. Pre-Christian Crosses
   Example: Tan cross, swastika
3. Saxon Crosses
   Example: Celtic or Irish Cross (upright cross with circle)
4. Russian Crosses
   Example: Slavic or Eastern Cross
5. Greek Crosses
   Example: (Cross of St. George) arms of equal length

BIBLIOGRAPHY

THE HOLY BIBLE

EARLY CHRISTIAN SYMBOLS IN GREAT BRITAIN—J. R. Allen

CHRISTIAN SYMBOLISM—Thomas Alfred Stafford

CHURCH SYMBOLISM—F. R. Webber

ANCIENT PAGAN SYMBOLS—Elizabeth Goldsmith

INDEX